Greta Thunberg
CLIMATE ACTIVIST

by Connor Stratton

FOCUS
READERS.

BEACON

www.focusreaders.com

Focus Readers is distributed by North Star Editions:
sales@northstareditions.com | 888-417-0195

Produced for Focus Readers by Red Line Editorial.

Photographs ©: Christian Charisius/dpa/AP Images, cover, 1; Shutterstock Images, 4, 7, 8–9, 10, 13, 14, 20, 22, 29; Jean-Christophe Bott/Keystone/AP Images, 16; Alik Keplicz/AP Images, 19; Jason DeCrow/AP Images, 25; Kirsty Wigglesworth/AP Images, 27

Library of Congress Cataloging-in-Publication Data
Names: Stratton, Connor, author.
Title: Greta Thunberg : climate activist / by Connor Stratton.
Description: Lake Elmo, MN : Focus Readers, [2021] | Series: Important
    women | Includes index. | Audience: Grades 4-6
Identifiers: LCCN 2020036700 (print) | LCCN 2020036701 (ebook) | ISBN
    9781644936924 (hardcover) | ISBN 9781644937280 (paperback) | ISBN
    9781644938003 (pdf) | ISBN 9781644937648 (ebook)
Subjects: LCSH: Thunberg, Greta, 2003---Juvenile literature. | Child
    environmentalists--Sweden--Biography--Juvenile literature. |
    Environmentalists--Sweden--Biography--Juvenile literature.
Classification: LCC GE56.T55 S77 2021 (print) | LCC GE56.T55 (ebook) |
    DDC 363.738/74092 [B]--dc23
LC record available at https://lccn.loc.gov/2020036700
LC ebook record available at https://lccn.loc.gov/2020036701

Printed in the United States of America
Mankato, MN
012021

About the Author

Connor Stratton writes and edits children's books. He loves poetry and history, especially by and about fierce women. Every day he works to be a better feminist. He lives in Minnesota.

Table of Contents

CHAPTER 1

Climate Strike 5

 TOPIC SPOTLIGHT

Climate Change 8

CHAPTER 2

Early Life 11

CHAPTER 3

Fridays for Future 17

CHAPTER 4

United Behind Science 23

Focus on Greta Thunberg • 28
Glossary • 30
To Learn More • 31
Index • 32

Climate Strike

August 20, 2018, was a Monday. Greta Thunberg had school that day. But the 15-year-old skipped class. Instead, she sat outside Sweden's **parliament**. She had a message for Sweden's leaders.

 Greta Thunberg stands outside the building where the Riksdag, Sweden's parliament, meets.

Greta cared about **climate change**. She knew countries could make changes that would help solve this problem. But Greta thought Sweden was not doing enough. She wanted Sweden's leaders to act.

So, Greta started a school **strike** for the climate. Sweden's elections

Did You Know?

Greta painted a sign for her strike. It said "School Strike for Climate" in Swedish.

 Students who joined Greta's strike often held signs with messages about the climate.

were in three weeks. She decided to skip every day of school until then.

At first, Greta sat all by herself. But more and more people joined her each day. Soon, she became known around the world.

Climate Change

Energy helps people survive around the world. People often burn **fossil fuels** for energy. These fuels power cars, lights, and much more. But they also create **greenhouse gases**. These gases are trapping too much heat on Earth. As a result, climate change is happening. Sea ice is melting. **Droughts** are getting worse. People and animals are dying.

Governments must act quickly. They must make huge changes. For instance, countries must stop using coal and gas. Instead, they can get power from the sun and wind. People can call for their leaders to make these changes.

Power plants are major sources of greenhouse gases.

Chapter 2

Early Life

Greta Thunberg was born on January 3, 2003. She grew up in Stockholm, Sweden. Greta's father is an actor. Her mother is a singer.

Greta first learned about climate change in school. She was eight.

 Greta became concerned about climate change at a young age.

Other students did not seem upset. But Greta felt very sad.

Greta is autistic. Autism is a medical condition. It shapes how people experience the world. It can affect how they learn and communicate with other people.

Many autistic people think differently, too. They may become very interested in certain subjects. For Greta, that subject was climate change. She learned more about how serious the problem was. And

If climate change leads to more droughts, millions of people could run out of food.

she saw that people were not doing enough to help. At age 11, Greta became **depressed**. She stopped speaking. She also stopped eating.

Greta wanted her family to stop eating meat and flying in airplanes.

When airplanes burn fuel, they release greenhouse gases into the air.

Planes make climate change worse. Raising animals for meat is an even bigger cause of climate change.

Greta's parents wanted to help her. So, they made those changes. Over time, Greta started to feel better. She felt like people were listening. And she felt like she could make a difference. She thought about other actions she could take.

In 2018, Greta got an idea. She would do a school strike. It would raise awareness about the climate. It would show Sweden's leaders they needed to act.

Did You Know?

Greta is related to the scientist who first figured out how greenhouse gases work.

Chapter 3

Fridays for Future

At first, Greta skipped every day of school. After Sweden's fall elections, she went to school four days a week. But she did a school strike every Friday. Greta posted about the strikes online.

 At many of her Friday strikes, Greta gave speeches to huge crowds.

Greta wanted Sweden to use less fossil fuel. Until that happened, she said she would keep skipping school. She also told other students to strike. She called the strikes Fridays for Future.

Around the world, students joined Greta on Fridays. In

Did You Know?

Greta often sends her speeches to scientists. They make sure all the facts are right.

The strikes called for leaders to make huge changes, such as stopping the use of coal.

November 2018, approximately 15,000 students skipped school in Australia. By December, strikes had spread to hundreds of cities across the world.

Thousands of students join Greta for a strike in Switzerland in January 2020.

Greta was doing more than skipping school. She also gave speeches about climate change. On December 4, 2018, Greta spoke to members of the **United Nations** (UN). She blamed the world's leaders for not taking action. Greta's speech spread quickly online. Millions of people watched and shared it.

Greta kept calling on leaders to act. In January 2019, Greta spoke to the world's top business leaders. In April, she spoke to the leaders of Europe. Meanwhile, school strikes around the world grew and grew.

Did You Know?

Approximately 1.4 million people joined one strike in March 2019. There were students from 123 countries.

Chapter 4

United Behind Science

Greta took the 2019–2020 school year off. She spent the time being an activist. She traveled and spoke about climate change. A big UN event took place in September 2019. Greta planned to speak at it.

Greta traveled by sailboat to protect the environment and raise awareness.

The event was in New York City. Greta came from Europe. But she didn't take a plane. Instead, she rode a boat. Greta sailed across the Atlantic Ocean. The trip took two weeks. But Greta wanted to show that climate change was a crisis. In a crisis, huge actions are needed.

When Greta reached New York, a climate strike took place. Four million people took part around the world. It was the largest climate event ever. A few days later, Greta

 Greta is known for showing her passion when she speaks.

spoke at the UN. She had harsh
words for the world's leaders.

Greta continued to travel, speak,
and strike. But in March 2020, a
virus spread around the world.

As a result, Greta paused the Friday strikes.

The virus and climate change had different causes. But they had some of the same solutions. In both cases, people had to **unite** behind the science. When people ignored scientists' warnings, both problems tended to get worse.

Did You Know?

In December 2019, Greta was named *Time* magazine's Person of the Year.

> **Greta believes people must take action now to protect the future.**

Greta knew the changes needed to stop climate change were huge. To some people, those changes seemed impossible. But science showed they were necessary.

FOCUS ON
Greta Thunberg

Write your answers on a separate piece of paper.

1. Write a paragraph summarizing Chapter 1.

2. Would you skip school to bring attention to an important problem? Why or why not?

3. How old was Greta when she did her first climate strike?

    A. 8 years old

    B. 11 years old

    C. 15 years old

4. Why has Greta used many of her speeches to speak out against world leaders?

    A. World leaders have all taken huge steps to reduce climate change.

    B. World leaders often have the most power to reduce climate change.

    C. World leaders can't affect climate change.

5. What does **activist** mean in this book?

*She spent the time being an **activist**. She traveled and spoke about climate change.*

    A. someone who acts to help make change

    B. someone who owns a business

    C. someone who rules a country

6. What does **awareness** mean in this book?

*It would raise **awareness** about the climate. It would show Sweden's leaders they needed to act.*

    A. the cause of a disease

    B. knowledge about a problem

    C. a choice to do nothing

Answer key on page 32.

Glossary

climate change
A human-caused global crisis involving long-term changes in Earth's temperature and weather patterns.

depressed
Having a medical condition of deep, long-lasting sadness or loss of interest.

droughts
Long periods of little or no rain.

fossil fuels
Energy sources that come from the remains of plants and animals that died long ago.

greenhouse gases
Gases in the air that trap heat from the sun.

parliament
A group of people who make laws.

strike
When people stop work or school as a way to demand change.

unite
To come together.

United Nations
A worldwide organization that promotes cooperation among countries.

To Learn More

BOOKS

Doeden, Matt. *Greta Thunberg: Climate Crisis Activist.* Minneapolis: Lerner Publications, 2021.

Harris, Duchess. *Environmental Protests.* Minneapolis: Abdo Publishing, 2018.

Thunberg, Greta. *No One Is Too Small to Make a Difference.* New York: Penguin Books, 2019.

NOTE TO EDUCATORS

Visit **www.focusreaders.com** to find lesson plans, activities, links, and other resources related to this title.

Index

A
airplanes, 13–14, 24
autism, 12

C
climate change, 6, 8,
    11–12, 14, 20, 23–24,
    26–27

F
fossil fuels, 8, 18
Fridays for Future, 18, 26

G
greenhouse gases, 8, 15

S
school strikes, 6, 15,
    17–19, 21, 26
scientists, 15, 18, 26
speeches, 18, 20
Sweden, 5–6, 11, 15,
    17–18

U
United Nations (UN), 20,
    23, 25

V
virus, 25–26

Answer Key: 1. Answers will vary; **2.** Answers will vary; **3.** C; **4.** B; **5.** A; **6.** B